KATHLEEN JIMENEZ

ENCOUNTERING
GOD

AN 8-WEEK DISCOVERY OF HOW
ORDINARY PEOPLE MEET THE EXTRAORDINARY LORD

SELF-PUBLISHING SERVICES BY

antioch
books

ANTIOCHBOOKSPUBLISHING.COM

ISBN: 979-8-9878969-1-4

Self-Publishing Services by: Antioch Books
antiochbookspublishing.com

This study is dedicated to my father,
Rev. Richard Allen Turner.
You instructed me to follow only the Lord in everything I do. Now that you are
enjoying the glories of heaven and His presence, I pick up the mantle to preach the
Gospel and make Disciples of all nations.
Love you, Dad.

TABLE OF CONTENTS

HOW TO USE THIS 8-WEEK STUDY

I'm so glad you've decided to join me on this journey to encountering God! Although this book can be used as a personal devotional, I wrote this 8-week study with group Bible studies in mind. Each chapter contains lessons, each with study questions to help you apply what you've just read. At the end of each chapter, you'll find a page for you to record your own personal notes.

This book was intended for use as follows:

THROUGHOUT EACH WEEK

Each group member, on his or her own time throughout the week, should read the assigned chapter. It is recommended that each group member read one section per day. However, feel free to tailor your pace to fit the needs of your group. Just be sure to finish the chapter before the next group meeting!
- It is important to be thoughtful and transparent with each answer.
- At the end of each chapter, feel free to use the *Notes* page to write down any additional thoughts, prayers, or questions that may arise throughout the week.

AT EACH GROUP MEETING

Each group is a bit different, so this part may vary from group to group. When you all come together, be prepared to review your answers to each question. If there is a group leader(s), he or she should encourage everyone to share something from their answers in each section.
- As a group member, you should not feel pressured to share anything you are not comfortable sharing. Share as much or as little as you like. But remember, your responses could encourage a fellow group member!
- As a group member, when you are not speaking, you should turn to your *Notes* page and be prepared to write down any insights you may gain from your fellow group members.

I pray this study is an encouragement to you!

CHAPTER 1

ABRAHAM
The Setup

God appeared to a descendent of Noah to set in motion a promise for all mankind. Once again, men had forgotten the Lord, but Abraham—though far from perfect—chose to leave the worship of foreign gods and began a relationship with the Creator of the Universe that had everlasting repercussions.

———

Just before I turned 23 years old, I felt the Lord leading me to join a particular Christian theater company. To do so, I left my family and friends and traveled by bus from Michigan to California. One friend decided to accompany me on my new adventure and help me get a job in Yosemite National Park for the summer. On the way, we stopped to rest in Colorado and stayed with a hospitable couple who were friends of hers. From there, we parted ways, and I went forward on my own. I had to completely trust God because I didn't know *anyone* where I was going! Following God's call completely altered the course of my life. For four years I toured the United States and Canada as an actress and singer. Near the end of my time with the company I met my husband. I would not be the person I am today had I not journeyed cross-country on that 2,000-mile adventure with the Lord!

In this chapter, we will investigate how some of the encounters Abram had with the Lord—and his obedience to the call of the Lord—changed the destiny of mankind.

THE CALL AND THE BLESSING

Read Genesis 11:31-12:5

In this passage God spoke to Abram, but we aren't told how it transpired. Did God appear to him? Did Abram hear an audible voice? Did it happen in a dream? Did he hear the voice of God in his mind or in his spirit? We only know that it was forceful enough for Abram to obey.

Although God's words to Abram are recorded *after* Terah and his family set out for Canaan, Genesis 12:1 states, "The Lord *had said* to Abram," (emphasis added). This gives the impression that Abram first heard the Lord while still living in Ur because the instructions were to leave his country, his people, and his father's household. But then his father decided to go with him and lead the expedition. After his first encounter with God, Abram was willing to leave his family and go to an unknown place simply because God said to go. He was instructed to take only Sarai with him, but because of Terah's insistence on going, the group ended up staying in Harran a number of years, delaying the plan of the Lord.

In that initial encounter between God and Abram, God gave him a call and a blessing—The Blessing. The words of this Blessing are repeated several times to Abram, and to his son and grandson, throughout the book of Genesis. As long as the family followed God, The Blessing stayed with them and prospered them.

Like Abram's experience, our own first encounter with God is when He speaks to each one of us. It may come through the words of a preacher or a good friend. He may give you a dream. He may speak through a book you read. You may hear His voice inside you and know that He has spoken.

God has a plan for your life. Sometimes that involves leaving a job, your family, or just a negative pattern of living. Well-meaning people around you can contribute to delays by offering opinions and advice like, *God wouldn't tell you to do that. You have a good job. You are near family; you won't have any support. Our people don't do things like that or think that way.* There may be instances where someone joins you because it seems fun and different. But he or she may eventually decide that being comfortable and in a familiar routine is better than taking a risk with God. Or someone may choose to part ways with you because the call came only to you, not that person.

It was not until after Terah's death that Abram started again on his original instruction to go to Canaan. Although there was delay, we know the Lord blessed Abram in Harran because the Bible tells us he accumulated possessions and people (see Genesis 12:5). God saw what was in Abram's heart, and He will see what is in your heart.

Abram kept faith in his heart concerning the words God had spoken to him and as soon as he was released from the ties to his father, he obeyed. Throughout the account of Abram's life, there are long periods of time with no record of him hearing from God. These times did not deter Abram from believing the promise originally spoken to him. Abram knew what God had spoken, he had faith that it was still God's plan, and he kept going in pursuit of that plan!

STUDY QUESTIONS

Has God ever spoken to you? If so, describe your experience. How did He communicate? If not, would you like Him to speak? What would you like Him to say?

_____

_____

_____

_____

_____

_____

_____

_____

_____

_____

_____

_____

_____

_____

_____

_____

_____

_____

_____

_____

_____

_____

_____

_____

_____

_____

_____

_____

_____

_____

_____

_____

THE COVENANT

Read Genesis 12:6-7 and 15:1-18

While Abram was in Canaan, the Lord appeared to him, and once again, we don't know if it was a physical manifestation, a vision, in a dream, or if it was some other kind of manifestation. However, we do know that he *saw* the Lord because of the word "appeared." The appearance of God and promise of land were apparently weighty enough to prompt Abram to build an altar to the Lord, "who had appeared to him" (see Genesis 12:7 NIV). In those days it was common practice to build an altar to worship or to create a memorial of a visitation of the Lord.

The next appearance is very clear: "After this the word of the Lord came to Abram in a vision" (see Genesis 15:1 NIV). This was a detailed vision, and it was richly descriptive of how the Lord showed Abram what was promised. These verses are not just a glimpse into Abram's experience with God; Genesis 15:6 has importance for us **today**! As we believe what the Lord shows us about Jesus, we are given His righteousness (see 2 Corinthians 5:21).

The Lord made a covenant with Abram; this is a promise that cannot be broken. Many cultures on earth understand the power and significance of covenant. Depending on the culture, a covenant may require specific rituals to be performed between individuals or groups of people. This passage shows that the shedding of blood was one of the required actions taken to enact God's covenant with Abram. God knew that Abram would not be able to keep his part of the covenant, so He put Abram in a deep sleep and performed both parts of the covenant ritual Himself. The firepot and torch represented the Father and Jesus walking in the blood. The Father and Jesus were making the covenant on behalf of Abram and his descendants.

Read Genesis 17:4-6, 15-16

The Lord appeared to Abram to continue with covenant rituals. This time it was the exchange of names. In Hebrew, the name of the Lord is YHWH. We say it as "YAH-WEH." God gave Abram the AH from His own name and changed Abram's name to Abra*h*am. The Lord also changed Sarai's name to Sarah, adding the H. But Abram wasn't the only one who received a new name. The Lord took on Abraham's name and, from then on, was called The God of Abraham. This change was not simply to exchange names but to change the meaning of names. "Abram" means *exalted father*. "Abraham" means *father of a multitude*. "Sarai" means *my princess* and "Sarah" means *princess to all the nations of the world*. God promised to make Abraham the father of many nations and Sarah the mother of nations and kings. That is quite a covenant!

STUDY QUESTIONS

**Have you ever made a covenant?
Did you know marriage is a covenant?**

_____
_____
_____
_____
_____
_____
_____
_____
_____
_____

**How has reading this passage helped you to under-
stand the power and significance of covenants for you?
Would you like to be in a covenant with God?**

_____
_____
_____
_____
_____
_____
_____
_____
_____
_____
_____
_____
_____
_____
_____

THE PROMISE OF A SON

Read Genesis 18:1-2, 10

God physically appeared to Abraham along with two angels. I find it interesting that Abraham seemed to know it was the Lord. The Jews say that Abraham was a hospitable man. We see he had food prepared for his guests. The Lord told Abraham and Sarah that they would have a son, even though Sarah had been unable to conceive and both she and Abraham were very old. It took several years, but the Lord kept his promise. Sarah gave birth to a son when she was 90 years old, and Abraham was 100 years old! Sarah named her son Isaac, which means "laughter." She was overjoyed that she could finally give Abraham a son!

When we read a promise in the Bible and take it as our own, we also rejoice when it is fulfilled. Isaac was a foreshadowing of Jesus. The Jews waited many years for the birth of the promised Son—the Messiah. When He was born, angels filled the sky with a joyful sound. The shepherds sought and found baby Jesus and rejoiced. Any time a promise or covenant of God is fulfilled, there is joy!

STUDY QUESTIONS

**What have you read in the Bible that brings you joy?
Describe a promise that the Lord gave you—or that
you took from His word—that He has fulfilled.**

_____
_____
_____
_____
_____
_____
_____
_____
_____
_____
_____
_____
_____
_____
_____
_____
_____
_____
_____
_____
_____
_____
_____
_____
_____
_____

THE SET UP

Read Genesis 22:1-18

God not only set up blessings for Abraham, He also used Abraham to set up The Blessing for us. By his willingness to sacrifice his son at the word of God, believing God would raise Isaac from the dead, he paved the way for God to sacrifice His son, Jesus, to redeem mankind from sin.

When God made Adam and Eve and placed them in the Garden of Eden, He gave them dominion, or stewardship, over the earth. They were not the owners, but they had the power to rule and the ability to decide what would happen on the earth. Even though the devil deceived them and caused them to go into spiritual death, he did not *take* their authority. They had to *give* it to him. God could no longer do just anything on earth. A human had to do it first, or decree that God would do it before the matter could take place. That is why Abraham had to be willing to sacrifice his son to God. Abraham's intent was enough for God to act by coming as a human to take the punishment for our sin.

Although human sacrifice was done in the worship of foreign gods, the Lord had never requested it. Abraham had to look to his many years of relationship with the Lord to trust Him in this. After all, Isaac was "the son of promise," meant to be his heir. If Isaac had died, there would have been no heir to the promise.

God will never ask us to sacrifice our children, but He will ask us to sacrifice our desires and dreams. When we give them to Him, willing to let them die, He takes them and resurrects them as something far better than we could have imagined. Sometimes He gives us a new desire that is the best for us and sometimes He takes the dream to a level beyond our own making. Our will must bow to His will for our lives. Abraham sacrificed many things and was given The Blessing in return.

15

STUDY QUESTIONS

In the ages to come, Abraham is referred to as "the father of faith." When we believe in salvation by Jesus, we become children of Abraham because we also gain righteousness by faith (see Romans 4:16). Since we have faith like Abraham, do you think we can have encounters like Abraham? Why or why not?

_____

_____

_____

_____

_____

_____

_____

_____

_____

_____

_____

_____

_____

_____

_____

_____

_____

_____

_____

_____

_____

_____

_____

_____

_____

MODERN EXAMPLE: RICK RENNER

Rick Renner and his family had a growing ministry, a lovely home, and a stable future. The Holy Spirit spoke to him to begin a church in Latvia and eventually Russia. Was it really God? Why would God ask him to leave his family roots, his home, and a thriving ministry, to take his wife and three sons to a nation on the other side of the world. That's crazy! Rick had to trust that he had heard the word of the Lord. Did everything go smoothly, proving it was God? NO!

They had many hardships because the devil did not want them to take the Gospel to that part of the world. Surely it was only missionary work for a few years. At least, that is what they thought. They have now been in ministry in that area of the world for over 30 years! Their three boys grew up and married Russian women. And although they maintain their US citizenship, Moscow is now their home.[1]

This kind of encounter changes not only the life of the believer and his or her immediate family, but it also impacts generations of others. Abraham was told, "in you all the families of the earth shall be blessed," (see Genesis 12:3 NKJV) Rick and Denise Renner have not only changed the future of their own family, but they have also impacted hundreds of thousands of lives all over the world with their obedience. Millions are reached through their books and Internet and television broadcasts.

Our obedience may not be setting us up to affect thousands, but we can be sure it will affect those with whom we come in contact, our family, our friends, and our co-workers. God always has good things in store for those who love Him. Jesus said, "But seek first the kingdom of God and His righteousness; and all these things will be added to you," (see Matthew 6:33 NKJV). "All these things" refers to the clothes, food, and provision mentioned in the earlier verses.

God has set apart the provision for everything we need. We are set up to succeed when we obey by seeking to do the work of the kingdom first.

---

1. "Unlikely" by Rick Renner, published by Harrison House

> ABRAM KNEW WHAT GOD HAD SPOKEN, HE HAD FAITH THAT IT WAS STILL GOD'S PLAN, AND HE KEPT GOING IN PURSUIT OF THAT PLAN!

CHAPTER 2

MOSES
Deliverance

I n order to prove Himself to His people, God often chooses leaders and gives them dramatic encounters. There is no room for doubt that it is the Lord Almighty communicating with them. Even with the great miracles that are witnessed, people are tough to deal with, and deliverance is not always as easy as it could be.

———

I have heard amazing accounts of God appearing to others. One of the first was back in the 1970s when I read a book that spoke of a church having powerful services with a visitation of the Holy Spirit. The pastor said that someone passing by the church building saw flames engulfing the roof, but nothing was burning. The spectator almost called the fire department but decided to walk into the church instead. We see a similar visitation to Moses.

THE STRANGE APPEARANCE

Read Exodus 3:1-6

Moses was a man whom God favored. He was a Hebrew who escaped death as a male slave by being raised in the household of the Pharaoh of Egypt. However, as an adult in line to be Pharaoh, he killed an Egyptian who had been mistreating a Hebrew slave. When Moses found out that the murder was witnessed, he ran away from Egypt and his call to help his people—but he couldn't run away from God. Even after 40 years, marriage and a family, and working as a shepherd for a Gentile, his call from God had not been rescinded.

Before you are born you are given a destiny to fulfill. God puts certain gifts and talents in you to help you carry out His plan for your life. He wants you to seek Him and know Him. Even when you make mistakes or, for a time, turn away from Him, He is always waiting for you to return. He does not take away your calling, but it may go unfulfilled.

If we were to brainstorm ways that God would appear to someone, I am certain no one would say, "How about if God sits on a bush with His glory so that the bush starts to burn but doesn't burn up!" This was such a strange occurrence that Moses had to go investigate. As he approached, God spoke to him from the bush and Moses actually answered Him! Most of us would have run away screaming. In this life-altering exchange, God told Moses who He is, and after realizing to whom he was speaking, Moses hid his face because he was afraid to continue looking.

STUDY QUESTIONS

Have you ever heard God speaking to you? Perhaps you have not heard Him audibly, but you have heard Him in your spirit. God will sometimes do things to get your attention because He wants you to know Him. He wants to give you His plan for your life. What are some interesting things God has said or done that made you stop and think about Him or talk to Him?

_____

_____

_____

_____

_____

_____

_____

_____

_____

_____

_____

_____

_____

_____

_____

_____

_____

_____

_____

_____

_____

_____

_____

_____

_____

THE PLAN

Read Exodus 3:7-15

Not only did God speak to Moses, a shepherd in a lonely desert, He gave Moses a grand plan. The Israelites had not heard from God since Joseph was alive, so Moses wanted to be sure they would listen to him when he told them he had a message from God. After committing murder, Moses ran away and thought the people might ask, "Why would God talk to you?"

The Lord introduced Himself to Moses with His mysterious name, "I AM WHO I AM," as a way to be identified. Then He gave the covenant name, "The God of Abraham, the God of Isaac, and the God of Jacob." God wanted His people to know that He remembered His covenant and would keep it.

God is referred to by many different names throughout the Old Testament. It is important for us as believers to know the different names of God because each name represents a distinct part of the covenant God has made with mankind. For instance, Jehovah Jireh (or Yahweh Yireh) means "the God who sees ahead and provides." God revealed this name when He provided a ram for the sacrifice, so Abraham would not have to kill Isaac. God's plan includes us depending upon His promises, and we have to know them to be able to use them.

STUDY QUESTIONS

Do you know any of the Biblical names of God? Some of the names are: Yahweh Yireh – The Lord my Provider, Yahweh Rohe – The Lord my Shepherd, Yahweh Rapha – The Lord my Healer, Yahweh Nissi – The Lord my Banner, Yahweh Tsidkinu – The Lord my Righteousness. Which one would you use to claim a promise for your life and why?

_____

_____

_____

_____

_____

_____

_____

_____

_____

_____

_____

_____

_____

_____

_____

_____

_____

_____

_____

_____

_____

_____

_____

Read Exodus 3:16-22

The Lord assured Moses that the Jewish elders would accept the plan. That was the easy part. God also knew that the Egyptians were not going to let their free slave labor walk away. God said He would punish the Egyptians in such a way that they would want to be rid of the Israelites. He also explained that just by asking, the Israelites would be able to leave Egypt with enough gold, silver, and goods to pay for all the wages of their captivity!

When God gives us a plan, there will be easy parts and there will be parts that require faith and courage. We must be sure that the Lord is directing us and that we are not simply following our own thoughts and ideas to accomplish something we want to do ourselves. He pays the way for His plan. Too many times, we don't start on a project the Lord gives because we don't have the money, but prayer and faith will show us where and how to begin. The Lord provides as we take action.

STUDY QUESTIONS

What plan or idea has the Lord given you that was bigger than you could do yourself? Did you obey and complete it? If you have not yet received an idea or plan, write a prayer of commitment to be willing to be used however God desires.

_____
_____
_____
_____
_____
_____
_____
_____
_____
_____
_____
_____
_____
_____
_____
_____
_____
_____
_____
_____
_____
_____
_____
_____
_____
_____

DELIVERANCE FROM EVIL TO POWERFUL GOOD

Read Exodus 19:1-13, 16-20

After completing the plan that he was given by God, and after being delivered from the Egyptian army by God giving them safe passage through the Red Sea, Moses and the Israelites arrived at Mount Sinai. Moses went up the mountain where God spoke to him again. He could not see God through the cloud, but he could clearly hear His voice. This time the Lord wanted all of Israel to hear Him. Keep in mind, these were not people who were used to movies with special effects and the wonders of modern technology. When they saw a huge, dark cloud descend upon the mountain with lightning coming from it, heard loud peals of thunder, and heard a trumpet (shofar or ram's horn) that was so loud every one of almost two million people could hear it—they reacted in fear. To top that, Moses spoke (without modern amplification) over the sound of the trumpet and God answered him!

I don't know about you, but I think I would be on the ground on my face at that point! Aren't we glad that God has now made Himself accessible through Jesus and the Holy Spirit? With reverence, we can speak to Him as we would a friend. Although He can, and sometimes does, speak to people in an audible voice, He usually speaks to our spirits with a quiet voice, much like our own thoughts.

STUDY QUESTIONS

Has God ever delivered you from a bad situation? Did you sense His power? How did you react?

_____

_____

_____

_____

_____

_____

_____

_____

_____

_____

_____

Why do you think Moses was not afraid to be close to God?

_____

_____

_____

_____

_____

_____

_____

_____

ENTERING THE PRESENCE OF GOD

Read Exodus 20:18-21 and 24:1, 9-11

In the verses before our reading, God gave Moses the Ten Commandments. We will focus on the events that occurred after they were given, but I suggest going back to read them another time.

Moses took the God-given commandments to the people, but they were so frightened that they told him to get the messages from God and relay them himself. They did not want to hear or see God. Their previous encounter with God made them want to separate from Him. The text does not tell us, but I would think God was disappointed.

The Lord extended the invitation to meet with Him beyond Moses to Aaron, his two sons, and 70 of the elders of Israel. These 74 men were allowed to go up the mountain. They saw into the throne room of Heaven and then ate a meal in the presence of God Himself! This is astonishing to me. Many of the same elders who saw the Lord, later joined in creating and worshipping an idol of Egypt. It seems impossible that they would do such a thing.

Seeing God Himself did not create faith in them to stay consistent in the hard time of waiting for Moses when he later stayed on the mountain for 40 days (see Exodus 32:1-6). I understand why Paul said, "We walk by faith, not by sight," (see 2 Corinthians 5:7 NKJV).

STUDY QUESTIONS

Have you ever seen a miracle, or a time when it was evident that God was moving? Describe it. Did you continue in faith for a long time because of what you saw?

_____

_____

_____

_____

_____

_____

_____

_____

_____

_____

_____

_____

If you were with a group of people that were offered the opportunity to be in the physical presence of the Lord, would you like to go, or would you want to appoint someone to represent you?

_____

_____

_____

_____

_____

_____

_____

MODERN EXAMPLE: WILLIAM SEYMOUR

William Seymour was the son of emancipated slaves in Louisiana. He came out of poverty and studied under Charles Parham, a well-known Pentecostal minister.[1] Under the direction of the Holy Spirit, Seymour traveled to Los Angeles and met with a small prayer group. The group had been praying for a move of God and had experienced what is known as the baptism of the Holy Spirit with speaking in other tongues. Under Seymour's leadership and teaching, their band of a few people kept growing until they were too big for the house where they were meeting.

To accommodate the increasing number of people, Seymour rented a two-story building on Azusa Street that had once been a stable. The people cleaned it out and started holding meetings. Years later, witnesses would describe a cloud of glory that would come down in the meetings. Young children would even play hide-and-seek in the mist. Praise and worship would go on for hours at a time. Teenagers would pray for people who came with infirmities, and see those same people leave healed.

William Seymour would pray in an upstairs room and not come down to preach until God said to go. Like Moses with the veil over his face (see Exodus 34:33-35), Seymour would put a box over his head and sit on the stage. He would not take it off even to preach. Because of his humility and obedience, and the faith of the people, great miracles happened. People would fall under the power of the Holy Spirit, sometimes for hours at a time. According to witnesses, one man even had a missing arm grow out![2] This movement lasted a few years, but then waned due to opposition from other Christian leaders.

Because of the Israelites' lack of faith, they wandered in the wilderness for 40 years. Who knows how long the mighty miracles would have continued had the Body joined together in

31

unity with the Los Angeles meetings?

We are now believing for a mighty move of God on the earth. Many have been enslaved by worldly patterns. There are pockets of miracles but no unified move of power. God is raising up His children to throw off the deception of the enemy. We will march into a new promised land of the blessing of the Lord.

---

1. https://en.wikipedia.org/wiki/William_J._Seymour

2. https://www.revival-library.org/revival_heroes/20th_century/seymour_william.shtml

> WHEN GOD GIVES US A PLAN, THERE
> WILL BE EASY PARTS AND THERE WILL
> BE PARTS THAT REQUIRE FAITH
> AND COURAGE.

CHAPTER 3

ISAIAH
The Promise

Old Testament prophets were given extraordinary visions of earth and Heaven. Isaiah saw both, going hundreds and thousands of years ahead in time. Much of what we understand about Heaven, the life and death of Jesus, and the coming millennium are found in the book of Isaiah—where God gave more of the promise of the Messiah.

———

Now that we have the ability to create movies with special effects, it would be wonderful to see someone portray the visions of the prophets in the Old Testament. The words of the Bible are very descriptive, and God gave us imagination, but today's world is visually oriented. Perhaps seeing these images would stimulate action in the body of Christ and in unbelievers. They would create more understanding of just how possible amazing encounters with the Lord truly are.

THE THRONE ROOM

Read Isaiah 1:1 and 6:1-4

Isaiah was chosen by God to be a prophet during the reign of four kings. It is interesting that the first verse describes the entire book of Isaiah as "The vision." He was given one cohesive vision from God that kept going for 66 chapters and spanned many years! His encounters with God were no less amazing than those of Abraham and Moses.

In chapter 6, when the first king he served under died, Isaiah was given a glimpse into Heaven and saw the Lord on His throne! The train of His robe was so long that it went around the entire throne room, which was later said to hold thousands and thousands of people. He also saw four amazing angels around the throne. Throughout the Bible, we see different kinds of angels and, in this vision, Isaiah saw the *seraphim*—the same ones that John described in Revelation 4:6-8. These are the only angels said to have six wings and they constantly worship the Lord. In Isaiah's vision. The angels' voices were so weighty that the sound vibrations shook the foundations of the temple.

This vision makes me think of something we might see in a movie, or experience in a special venue like Universal Studios. For us it would be awesome and exciting, but for someone like Isaiah it must have been terrifying. Although I am sure he was not allowed to see the Lord's face, seeing His glory on the throne and creatures like none on earth would have been overwhelming.

STUDY QUESTIONS

Have you ever been given a glimpse of the physical glory of God? Have you ever felt overwhelmed by His presence? Describe a time in your life when either of those occurrences happened to you or how you think you would react if they did?

_____
_____
_____
_____
_____
_____
_____
_____
_____
_____
_____
_____
_____
_____
_____
_____
_____
_____
_____
_____
_____
_____
_____
_____

Read Isaiah 6:5-8

Of course, Isaiah lived before the atoning sacrifice of Jesus. He lived under the Law of Moses, which made people extraordinarily conscious of their sin. Even though Isaiah followed God and lived by faith as a prophet, seeing the Lord on His throne brought Isaiah under a deep conviction. It is interesting that he described the sinful state as being "of unclean lips." One reason could be what Jesus said, "For out of the abundance of the heart, the mouth speaks," (see Matthew 12:34 NKJV). When there is sin in our hearts it will come out of our mouths.

The other thing to note is that the seraph cleansed Isaiah's lips with a live coal from the altar and stated, "your sin is atoned for." We know only the blood of Jesus paid for our sin, so how was it possible to atone for Isaiah's sin before Jesus' time? The coal was pulled from the altar in Heaven, but it is important to remember that Heaven does not exist in time. That altar was the very same altar where the blood of Jesus was sprinkled when He gave his life for ours. In chronological earth-time, Jesus' sacrifice occurred *after* Isaiah's experience but, ultimately, that fact is irrelevant. Heaven operates outside the confines of time, so it was still the blood of Jesus that took away Isaiah's sin. According to Revelation 13:8, Jesus was slain from the foundation of the world.

This part of the vision ended in verse 8 with a question from the Lord followed by a message. The Lord asked, "Whom shall I send?" God needed a messenger who was willing to speak His words to the people. Some of the words were of judgement and hard to hear, but the Lord always leaves a way out of the punishment if people will repent and obey Him. That was the commission of every prophet, and many were reviled or killed for it. Still, Isaiah responded, "Here am I. Send me!"

STUDY QUESTIONS

Can you imagine seeing a seraph? How would your reaction be different from that of Isaiah?

_____
_____
_____
_____
_____
_____
_____
_____
_____
_____
_____

Have you been convicted of your sin? Have you repented and received Jesus as your Lord and Savior? Jesus took the punishment for our sin on the cross and shed His blood. God now asks every person, not just prophets, "Who will go for us?" What is your answer?

_____
_____
_____
_____
_____
_____
_____
_____

THE SIGN OF A SON

Read Isaiah 7:13-16

Isaiah was now under King Ahaz, the grandson of Uzziah. The kings of Aram and Israel were teaming up to fight Judah and Ahaz was afraid. God sent Isaiah to the king with a message of support. The Lord told Ahaz to ask for a sign to prove that support. Ahaz, probably thinking he was doing well by quoting Moses, refused to put the Lord to the test. However, it was God's request for the sign to be chosen. Since Ahaz disobeyed, God gave His own sign that would not be fulfilled until long after the captivity of Israel. It is here we first hear about the virgin birth and the name "Immanuel".

The Lord goes on to say that as a young child, the boy will know right from wrong. We know from the gospels that Jesus grew in the favor of God and men (see Luke 2:52). From history we know that the kingdoms of Aram and Israel were destroyed, along with Judah, hundreds of years before Jesus was born. God kept His promise but not in an expected way.

Read Isaiah 9:2-3, 6-7

Again, in his descriptive narrative, Isaiah spoke more words about the Messiah. When Jesus began His ministry, the Jewish people were no longer in charge of their nation. They were occupied by Rome. They were also in the darkness of a religious spirit. God had not spoken to them through a prophet for 400 years. His glory had departed from the temple. They were ruled by pagan governors and priests who cared more for themselves than for their flock. The Jewish leaders kept the letter of the law but not the spirit of the love of God for His people. They also added many regulations not given by God.

Jesus came in the power of the Holy Spirit and brought back the light of the glory of God.

Isaiah described the government as being on the Messiah's shoulders. That is why people thought the Messiah would come to overthrow Rome and set up an earthly kingdom. What hope-filled words these must have been for the Jews. In these verses, the Messiah is called "Mighty God, Everlasting Father." Did they understand that this was God saying He would come as a man to right the eternal wrong and do what no human born in sin could do?

STUDY QUESTIONS

When you read these verses, how do they make you feel? Describe a time when you experienced being in a kind of darkness, needing the light of deliverance.

_____

_____

_____

_____

_____

_____

_____

_____

_____

_____

What do you understand about the titles of Jesus in verse 6?

_____

_____

_____

_____

_____

_____

_____

_____

_____

THE SUFFERING SERVANT

Read Isaiah 52:13-53:6

Because we know that Isaiah received most of his revelations in a vision, it would be wonderful to know what he saw for these verses. He mixed the ministry of Jesus with the crucifixion. He stated that the servant will be wise, or prosperous, highly exalted, and then described how Jesus looked after he was beaten. The text goes back to his youth, early ministry, and then to the cross again.

At the beginning of the chapter, I mentioned movies. Mel Gibson directed a stunning portrayal of the crucifixion in "The Passion of the Christ." In this film, we see on screen what I believe is a close representation of what Isaiah saw in his vision. Images are powerful!

Verse 5 of chapter 53 is one of the most quoted verses today. The apostle Peter gave a loose quotation of verses 4-6 in the second chapter of his first letter. Why is this so important? They describe the physical action that took place to right a spiritual wrong. Today many might call someone like Isaiah a false prophet because he did not see the fulfillment of his prophecy. It came hundreds of years later when the Word of God took on human flesh. This was the promise that the Jews clung to through all the tragedies that came from their disobedience. When Jesus was crucified, some thought He was being punished by God for blasphemy. They did not understand His perfection. Every beating, piercing, and crushing was done to reverse the curse that Adam had put us under. Jesus had done nothing to deserve His death. He took that on for us. His punishment brought us peace. That word in Hebrew is "shalom." It means *safety, prosperity, well-being, intactness, wholeness, security, contentment, and good health.* Every one of those definitions are promises that belong to us if we choose to give our lives to Jesus.

STUDY QUESTIONS

What do you see when you read these verses? Ask the Father to give you an image of all that Jesus took on for us.

_____

_____

_____

_____

_____

_____

_____

Jesus said that He came to give us His peace (see John 14:26-27). How are you living in His peace, wholeness, rest, prosperity, and health?

_____

_____

_____

_____

_____

_____

Have you, or has anyone you know had a vision from God? If so, describe what you saw or what was told to you.

_____

_____

_____

_____

_____

_____

_____

THE JUBILEE

Read Isaiah 61:1-3

Jesus went to a synagogue and was asked to do the pre-scribed weekly reading. These are the words He read, stopping just after the beginning of verse 2. The Lord showed Isaiah the purpose of Jesus' ministry. Jesus told the congregation that they were seeing the fulfillment of this prophecy. It was no coincidence He read those verses.

Isaiah had to give many discouraging words to Israel, but he was also blessed to give them the answer to their troubles. His prophecies gave the promise of the Lord to send a Savior who would come in the fullness of time. Isaiah said the Messiah would proclaim the year of the Lord's favor—the year of Jubilee—a set time that God gave to Moses for the Jews to keep. It was to be a time when captives were set free and when land was to be returned to the original owner or his family. It would help eradicate poverty and produce justice. Jesus declared a spiritual Jubilee. We were set free from the captivity of our sin and God received back His "property," His people.

STUDY QUESTIONS

What do these verses mean to you? How would a Jubilee year affect you today?

_____
_____
_____
_____
_____
_____
_____
_____
_____
_____
_____
_____
_____
_____

Did you know that if you are in Christ, you are anointed by the Lord to proclaim the Gospel and that you are commissioned to also fulfill these words? What have you done that would be considered as proclaiming the good news?

_____
_____
_____
_____
_____
_____
_____
_____
_____
_____

MODERN EXAMPLE: EMMA STARK

Emma is a prophet who lives in Glasgow, Scotland. She and her husband, David, lead the Glasgow Prophetic Alliance. God called her as a prophet to the nations. She has had many visions, dreams, and messages from the Lord. This is a quote from her book, *The Prophetic Warrior*, about her first encounter with an angel.

> *"As a passionate eighteen-year-old I would run back from my lecture classes at university and fall onto my knees on my bedroom floor, reading Isaiah 6 and the description of how his lips were burned by the burning coals. For days I would get like this and beg God to do the same to me. One day a being, a* **seraphim**, *walked into the room with tongs and burned my lips. My mouth physically became ulcerated and bleeding inside. (I still have the Bible that I bled over that day). In pain, I went to my minister for help. He poured me a glass of water, blessed it, and I drank it. My mouth healed as quickly as it had begun to bleed."[1]*

The Lord uses Emma to encourage people in their destiny. He also uses her to warn people who are walking in disobedience to return to the path of God. She prays for people and sees the Lord perform miracles. Her church trains prophets and seers in their callings so that they function in keeping with the truth of the Bible.

Like Isaiah, Emma has seen the throne room of God and has been overcome by the love and majesty of the Father. She has been cheered and reviled and knows that the path of a prophet is not easy. Her desire is to see that every believer learn to live and walk in the Spirit, being able to discern between good and evil, to act in the power of the Holy Spirit as Jesus desired for us.

STUDY QUESTIONS

When you read about someone like Emma, who has supernatural encounters with God, how does it make you think and feel? Do you believe her? Would you like something like that to happen to you? We are created as a spirit, given a physical body to live on the earth, and a soul that is comprised of a mind, will, and emotions. We have physical, intellectual, and emotional encounters. Should we not have spiritual encounters?

_____
_____
_____
_____
_____
_____
_____
_____
_____
_____
_____
_____
_____
_____
_____
_____
_____
_____
_____

---

1. "The Prophetic Warrior" by Emma Stark, published by Destiny Image.

Notes

JESUS DECLARED A
SPIRITUAL JUBILEE. WE WERE SET
FREE FROM THE CAPTIVITY OF OUR
SIN AND GOD RECEIVED BACK HIS
"PROPERTY," HIS PEOPLE.

CHAPTER 4

MARY
The Fulfillment

Thousands of years in the past, God promised a savior for His people. The promise was repeated by the prophets. Then, 400 years of silence. When God spoke again, it was first to a priest, and then to a teenage girl who, like her ancestors before her, had to accept her part of the promise.

————

We read about angel encounters numerous times in the Bible. Angels carry the atmosphere of heaven because they come from God. Meeting an angel is almost as startling to humans as an encounter with God because we rarely focus on our spirit nature. In previous chapters, we saw the reactions of adult men who encountered angels. What happened when a holy angel appeared to a young girl?

THE CHOSEN ONE

Read Luke 1:26-38

About 700 years after the prophecies of Isaiah, and after about 400 years of silence, God sent the angel Gabriel to Nazareth. Gabriel is the same angel who was sent to the prophet Daniel and to Zechariah, father of John the Baptist. He also appeared to a girl named Mary, with great news. She was highly favored by the Lord and was chosen to bear the Messiah, to bring him into the world.

If you read Luke 1:11-12, you see that Gabriel's appearance to Zechariah in the temple filled the priest with great fear. In contrast, Mary, who was most likely 13 or 14 years old, the age at which Jewish girls were given in marriage, was troubled by the *words* the angel spoke, not by his appearance. Zechariah was a priest of the Lord who served at the temple. You would think, of all people, he would be overjoyed to see an angel. Mary, on the other hand, was a simple Jewish girl. It appears that Zechariah went through religious motions but had no sense of the Lord in his life. Of the two, she should have had the most fear. What was special about Mary?

Rick Renner did research on the writings of early church fathers and historians and found that Mary's father had the position of keeper of the scrolls in a synagogue. Because his wife was barren, they prayed for a child and, similar to Hannah in the Old Testament, promised to dedicate this child to the Lord. When Mary was born, they kept their promise by training her in Jewish history and law. They told her she would be used of the Lord, so she grew up expecting God to do something with her life.[1]

STUDY QUESTIONS

How do you think you would react if an angel appeared to you? Mary was very young but willingly gave herself to the plan of God. If an angel announced a plan to you that would require some sacrifice, what would your answer be?

_____

_____

_____

_____

_____

_____

_____

_____

_____

_____

_____

_____

_____

Whether you were raised in church or not, what do you expect God to do with your life?

_____

_____

_____

_____

_____

_____

_____

_____

STUDY QUESTIONS CONTINUED ON FOLLOWING PAGE

Another difference between Mary and Zechariah is that in verse 18, Zechariah challenged the angel's statement to him. He asked, "How can I be sure of this?" or "How shall I know this?" In other words, he asked the angel for proof because those were pretty outlandish words to say to an old man and woman. This man was a priest who had memorized much of the Old Testament. He should have been aware of the miracles where God gave children to barren women. Think of Sarah and Abraham!

On the other hand, Mary's question was not requesting proof, she just didn't understand how it would happen. The Lord knew her heart and allowed the angel to explain. Her response demonstrated the reason she was chosen. Fully aware of the danger of being unwed and pregnant, she humbly accepted the Word of the Lord through the angel. Mary recognized her purpose.

STUDY QUESTIONS (CONTINUED)

How do you think you would react if an angel appeared to you? Mary was very young but willingly gave herself to the plan of God. If an angel announced a plan to you that would require some sacrifice, what would your answer be? Whether you were raised in church or not, what do you expect God to do with your life?

_____

_____

_____

_____

Has God ever made an outlandish promise to you? If so, did you receive it even if you did not understand how it would be accomplished, or did you ask Him for proof?

_____

_____

_____

Are you aware of the many promises in the Bible that God has given to all of us? Jesus said that if we believe we receive and don't doubt, we can have any promise (see Mark 11:23-24). What promise would you like to receive?

_____

_____

_____

What purpose do you believe God has for you?

_____

_____

_____

THE SEED IS PLANTED

Read Luke 1:30-45

Immediately after her encounter with the angel, Mary visited Elizabeth, the wife of Zechariah.
She was unaware that the seed of the Word she accepted had already begun to grow within her. These two women were related by blood, and now also by miraculous children. Can you picture this scene? In the womb of his mother, John recognized the presence of the Messiah and leapt for joy! The Holy Spirit came upon Elizabeth, and she recognized Him also! She was given a word of knowledge about Mary's pregnancy and declared the baby to be the Lord. She then declared that Mary was blessed for believing in the Word of the Lord that was spoken to her.

Read Luke 1:46 - 55

Mary left one supernatural encounter and walked right into another! No one else in her time was being given words of knowledge and wisdom, especially women. Did she realize at this point how extraordinary her life would be? Also moved by the Holy Spirit, Mary began to sing a prophetic song. It was the first prophecy uttered by a human in the New Testament. These verses record that women were the first in the New Testament to exhibit Gifts of the Holy Spirit. Mary was overwhelmed with joy, gratitude, and amazement at what the Lord was doing and her part in it. Her purpose was far beyond her imagination. Both women gave themselves over to being used by the Spirit of God.

It would have been amazing to witness their meeting.
In 1 Corinthians 12:7-11, Paul outlined and defined the nine gifts of the Holy Spirit. Mary and Elizabeth exhibited several of them: the word of wisdom, the word of knowledge, and the gift of prophecy. Paul says they are for everyone.

STUDY QUESTIONS

Tell of a time you exercised a gift of the Spirit. If you have never had the experience, which ones would you like to be used in?

_____

_____

_____

_____

_____

_____

_____

_____

_____

_____

_____

_____

Describe a time when you were so overwhelmed by the joy or love of God that you had to sing or shout your praise to Him.

_____

_____

_____

_____

_____

_____

_____

_____

_____

_____

_____

MODERN EXAMPLE: SUSANNA WESLEY

Although Mary is the only woman who will ever birth and raise our Savior, there are other women who have given their lives to God to birth and raise ministers. One such woman is Susanna Wesley. As she was born in 1669, you might not think of her as modern, but she was progressive in her beliefs on education and instructed her daughters in the same manner as her sons.

Susanna married Samuel Wesley, an Anglican minister, and bore 19 children—10 of whom survived to adulthood. She was well educated from home schooling and home schooled her own children. Her most famous son was John Wesley, founder of the Methodist movement. His brother, Charles, wrote many hymns that are still sung in churches today. Susanna ran a tight ship in her household and was praised by John as a shining example of a Christian woman.

She was known for spending at least two hours per day in prayer and fellowship with the Lord. Often this was done in the presence of her children who were working on lessons. She would throw her long apron up over her head and create a private "tent of meeting" where she would pray and converse with God. The children knew not to disturb her while she was in the Lord's presence. This diligence and her knowledge of the Bible led her to have a Bible class for her children on Sunday afternoons. Neighbors heard about it and asked to join. At one time she had as many as 200 people attending.[2]

We often think that God only appears to famous men and women or only uses people who have many degrees or are well off financially. Both Mary and Susanna had training but not the kind the world admires. They were willing vessels for the Lord's use and did not seek notoriety.

Raising children who would change the world was their life's work. God considers that of extreme importance and blesses that work with His presence. Staying at home with your children should never be seen as a menial task. You are preparing the next generation.

---

1. Christmas: The Rest of the Story, 2022 Rick Renner

2. https://faithgateway.com/blogs/christian-books/praying-example-susanna-wesley/2

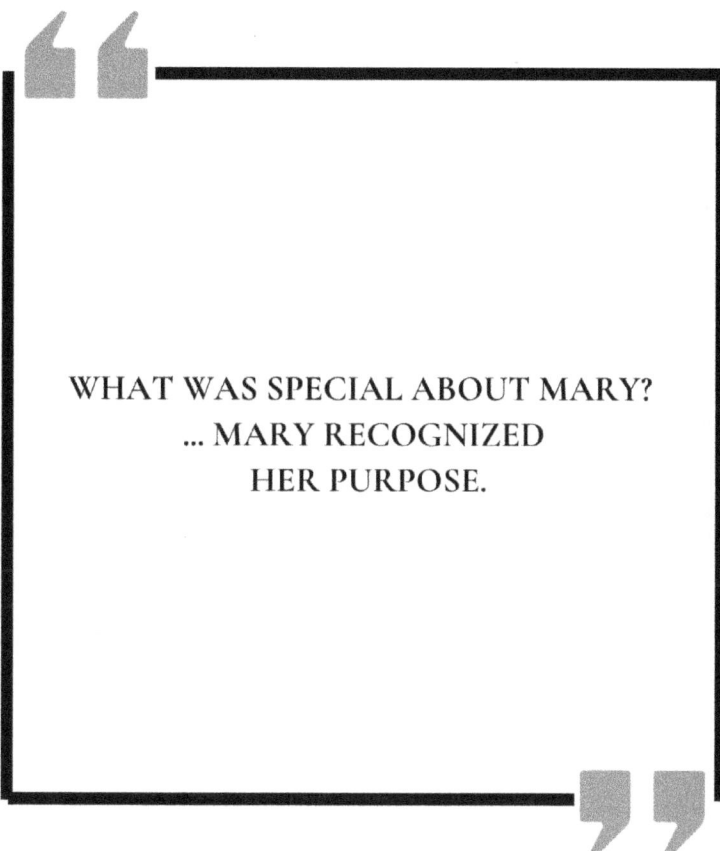

WHAT WAS SPECIAL ABOUT MARY?
... MARY RECOGNIZED
HER PURPOSE.

CHAPTER 5

THE DISCIPLES
The Call

In this chapter, we will read of a group of men who encountered Jesus separately—yet together. They were unique among all the followers of Jesus. It was to them the secrets of the Kingdom of God were first given. We can look at their lives to find how we should react when the call to follow Jesus is given.

———

How is your life going? Is everything running about the way you thought it should, or are you stuck in a routine, wondering how you got there and how you can get out. Even if things are pretty good, did you ever wonder if there was something more? Perhaps you feel something is just beyond your reach, but you can't quite grasp it.

I have often felt like there was more I should be doing. I would hear conflicting statements, such as, "Don't jump ahead of God! Wait on Him," and "Stop waiting around for something to happen! Find out what God is doing and join in!" So, which is it? Like our subjects in this chapter, I believe we should do what we know to do and be ready to go when He calls.

MANY ARE CALLED

Read Matthew 4:12-17, 23-25, and Mark 3:13-19

After Jesus had been baptized and had overcome temptation, He took up John's message, "Repent, for the Kingdom of Heaven is near." Before then, no one knew who He was except His family and coworkers. At the appropriate time, God released Him to begin His ministry. Think of it this way—until He was 30 years old, He followed His father Joseph and worked a trade. He was obedient to the Law of Moses. He helped His family and friends. He lived a normal life that honored God. There was a proper time for God to give new directions for Him to fulfill His destiny.

If we don't yet have a directive from God to do something different, we should use the talents He gave us to the best of our ability. If you are parents of young children, you know by the Word of God to raise them in the precepts of the Lord. If you are single, you should work to do good with your talents and help the church and the poor. When God sees that you are faithful in the basics, He will give you more responsibility.

The gospel of John states that it was the custom of Jesus to attend different synagogues, where He would be asked to speak. [Note: Jesus regularly attended services. If He did that, we should, also. That is a good place to start.] Whenever He spoke, He got the attention of the people and once the healings began, the crowds followed Him. They had heard many itinerant teachers, but Jesus was different. Even though they didn't know what it was, they recognized the anointing of God on Him. From the many, a few were chosen. Jesus heard His Father select the 12 who were to be known as His disciples. Most of the crowds were there out of curiosity and to see the miracles. Jesus' call to the apostles was received differently. His teaching had affected them so profoundly that they were willing to give up everything in their lives to follow Him. This is equivalent to what we saw in Abraham, who trusted the call of God strongly enough to leave everything he knew in order to be obedient.

While it is true that there will never again be "Apostles of the Lamb," those who walked physically on earth with Jesus and gave up their lives for the Gospel, everyone is called to follow Jesus. He told the apostles to "go and make disciples." Converts hear a good sermon and are convinced in their thinking. When pressure from this life or another interesting doctrine comes along, they can be easily swayed from their decision. Disciples give up their way of life to intensely follow Jesus and strictly adhere to His teaching. They choose to experience God on His terms, not how they think He should be. They do not chase after the waves of popular opinion. The Holy Spirit enlightening the Word of God is their standard.

Jesus ministered under the old covenant and fulfilled it, meaning He kept all of it. He did not do this so we could ignore the Old Testament instructions; it was to take on Himself our punishment for failing to keep the law (since He was blameless) and allow the Holy Spirit to bring our spirits from death to life and dwell in us. The Holy Spirit prompts us to keep the commands from the positive side. We do good because we love God and are grateful, not because we fear punishment. We dwell in Him and He dwells in us. We are His sheep; we hear His voice when He speaks to us.

STUDY QUESTIONS

Were you convinced in your thinking, or have you accepted Jesus as Savior in your heart? Describe your "born again" experience:

_____
_____
_____
_____
_____
_____
_____
_____
_____
_____
_____
_____

What does it mean to make Jesus the Lord of your life?

_____
_____
_____
_____
_____
_____
_____
_____
_____
_____
_____
_____

FEW CHOOSE THEIR CALLING

Read Luke 5:27-28, 18:18-24, and 19:1-10

These passages describe the two reactions to the call of Jesus. You can respond positively or negatively. Matthew Levi, the tax collector, considered a sinner by most Jews, immediately left his questionable profession when asked to follow Jesus. In the presence of the man who was holy and compassionate, of whom he had certainly heard much, Levi chose to turn away from colluding with the Romans and go toward a life of obedience and servanthood.

Although the Bible does not say so, we might reasonably guess that Levi did something similar to what Zacchaeus did in making restitution for cheating people. Jesus did not call Zacchaeus to follow Him, but He did go to his house for a meal (see Luke 19:1-10). Again, in the presence of the Anointed One, the chief tax collector repented of his sin and promised to give to the poor half of his possessions. Amazingly, he also said he would repay four times any amounts received by cheating.

Both of these men had complete changes of heart and were willing to give up wealth in order to dedicate themselves to God. The power of the Gospel is enough to overcome the pull of the things of this world. However, we have free will and each of us must choose whom we will serve.

In contrast, the man often known as the rich young ruler came to Jesus claiming to be a righteous person. When Jesus listed several of the 10 commandments, the man said he had kept them all since he was a child. Did you ever notice that Jesus did not say, "You shall have no other gods before me," or "You shall not covet"? The young man seemed to be unaware that he had a problem with those two commandments. Jesus gently points to them by asking the man to separate himself from his property and wealth and give all to the poor. He then issues the call to follow Him.

Unlike the tax collectors, this encounter ended with the man sadly walking away. His belongings and wealth had a hold on him from which he could not break free at that time. Jesus even stated that it is very difficult for the rich to enter the Kingdom of God. Some people use this example to claim that no Christian should be wealthy. However, the gospels also state that wealthy women supported Jesus and the disciples. Wealth is a tool to be used, not a treasure to be hoarded. The point of this lesson is that when you choose to answer the call to follow Jesus, everything must be laid before God. He knows your heart and may or may not require you to give up wealth, possessions, habits, and even people. As a loving Father, He will provide what you need for your journey with Him.

It is interesting to note that some scholars believe the unnamed young ruler of the gospels was actually Barnabas, named in the book of Acts. Either way, His encounter with Jesus changed his perspective of wealth.

STUDY QUESTIONS

Describe an area of your life that Jesus called you to walk away from when you accepted Him:

_____
_____
_____
_____
_____
_____
_____
_____
_____
_____
_____

What have you gained by choosing to follow Jesus?

_____
_____
_____
_____
_____
_____
_____
_____
_____
_____
_____

WHY THEY FOLLOWED

Read Matthew 4:18-22, John 1:35-42, and Luke 5:1-11

If you only read the calling of the first disciples from Matthew and Mark you might think that the fishermen were out in their boats one day casting nets, when a stranger came by and said "Follow me. I will make you fishers of men." They were so taken with the stranger that they immediately dropped everything and went with him. Really? Isn't that a bit far-fetched—even for the Gospel? The passages in John and Luke explain more of the circumstances. After all, Paul also said that faith comes by hearing (see Romans 10:17).

In John 1:35-42, we discover that Andrew had been a disciple of Jesus' cousin, John, the baptizer. It was John who pointed to Jesus as the Lamb of God. Andrew spent a day with Jesus and heard Him teach, then told Simon about Him. Jesus had already been in many synagogues in the Galilee area, preaching His message, and even without the modern conveniences of internet and cell phones, word quickly spread about this new rabbi.

After one of his synagogue appearances, Jesus went to Simon's home. While there, He healed Simon's mother-in-law. Surely that made quite an impression! In a couple of hours, the entire village must have heard because the Bible says people brought many who had various diseases to Simon's home. Jesus healed all of them and cast out many demons. Simon was watching all of this. I imagine that what Andrew told him was circling in his mind—that Jesus was the Messiah, the Lamb of God.

Fishermen were hard-working and rough. The final straw that broke through Simon's hard exterior was after he lent his boat to Jesus for a sermon. He could hear the message as he was cleaning his nets. Although he was exhausted, when Jesus told him to go out once again for a cast, he grudgingly obeyed. He was possibly remembering that Jesus had already done a lot for his family and village. Simon's obedience caused such a harvest of fish that he had to call James and John to bring their boat to help. The catch was abundant, overflowing, and miraculous. Simon knew he had been overwhelmingly blessed by the goodness of God through Jesus, even though his attitude stunk.

It was the composite of all these encounters that caused Simon to bow before Jesus and hand over control of his life. It was similar for Andrew, James, and John. They heard, saw, felt, and perceived in their spirits the power of the Holy Spirit on the Son of God. They were unable to deny their experiences and chose to answer "yes" to the call to follow the Messiah

STUDY QUESTIONS

What did you hear, see, and perceive about Jesus that caused you to say yes to His call?

_____

_____

_____

_____

_____

_____

_____

_____

_____

_____

_____

_____

_____

_____

_____

_____

_____

_____

_____

_____

_____

_____

_____

_____

WE GIVE THE CALL

Read John 1:43-50

Jesus "found" Philip. The Bible doesn't say He was walking along, and Philip happened to be in His path. We only find something if we have been looking for it. The Father sent Jesus to look for another disciple. Philip was discovered on the road to Galilee. God had a purpose for him, and Jesus issued the call. It makes me think of the parable of the lost sheep (see Matthew 18:12-13). God searches for those who belong to Him, for those whose hearts are open to Him.

As soon as he chose to follow Jesus, Philip went to find his friend, Nathanael. He had such good news that he wanted to share it. Nathanael was "found." Philip told Nathanael, "We have *found* the one Moses wrote about in the Law" (emphasis added). He said that because for hundreds of years the Jews had been waiting for the Messiah. They were looking for a savior.

Three times within three verses, God uses the words "finding" or "found," depending on the translation you read. People were seeking God. God was seeking disciples. In Matthew 7:7-8, Jesus tells us that everyone who seeks will find. You may think that you have been seeking certain things or opportunities or people and you haven't found them yet. Jesus depended on the Holy Spirit to tell Him where to seek. Perhaps you are not looking in the proper place, or it is not the proper time. God places great emphasis on seeking Him. In Matthew 6:33, Jesus tells us to seek the Kingdom of God first—before anything else—then other things will be given. When our lives are set in proper order, by following the Holy Spirit, we will find what we seek. God says in Jeremiah 29:13 that you will find Him when you seek Him with all your heart. Why haven't you found what you are seeking yet? Perhaps you first need to seek God more diligently.

When you find Him, you will be in the proper place and time to be shown how to find the rest.

Philip sought Nathanael to share the good news about Jesus. Andrew told Simon, and James and John learned by being around Andrew and Simon. They hardly knew Jesus, but they were already evangelists. Throughout the gospels, many people told others about what Jesus had done for them. In fact, a few times Jesus asked someone *not* to tell others because of the crowds that would inevitably gather, but the news was usually too good to keep silent.

We need to be telling others about Jesus. You might be concerned that your faith will be rejected. Nathanael scoffed at the idea that anything good could come from Nazareth, but Philip ignored that and insisted Nathanael see for himself. Jesus then gave Nathanael a word of knowledge from the Holy Spirit. Jesus said He saw him under the fig tree before Philip spoke to him. Those words shook Nathanael and caused him to declare that Jesus was the son of God and the King of Israel! His first encounter with Jesus was to be made aware that God knew who he was. Many people just need to be shown that God knows them and loves them. We are the vessels for that call.

STUDY QUESTIONS

How will your friends, neighbors, coworkers, and relatives learn about the love of the Father if you don't tell them? Part of our calling is to extend the call beyond ourselves. We are included in the process. What have you been seeking that you have not yet found? Did you try to find it before seeking the Father?

_____

_____

_____

_____

_____

_____

Have you shared the Gospel in the last 3 months? If so, with whom? If not, why not?

_____

_____

_____

_____

_____

_____

What encounter have you had with God that you want to share with others?

_____

_____

_____

_____

_____

_____

MODERN EXAMPLE: JESSE DUPLANTIS

Jesse Duplantis grew up around New Orleans, Louisiana. His family was extremely poor. He was raised to be tough because life was hard. Gangs and ambition for money drove his early life. He grew up Catholic but was kicked out of Catechism class because of his behavior. Later, his mother received salvation and started praying for her children. Jesse became a rock musician and was making a good living, but his lifestyle was filled with drugs and alcohol. His wife Cathy was saved and she also prayed for him.

As Jesse has described many times throughout the years, he was saved in the bathroom of a hotel room in Boston, Massachusetts. He and Cathy and their small daughter were there because he had a job playing concerts. Billy Graham was holding a crusade that was broadcast on television and Cathy asked him to watch the crusade with her. He made fun of it and asked why. Cathy said, "He draws more people than you." That caused Jesse to stop and think. Billy *did* draw large crowds, so he watched to see if he could figure out why. Billy Graham's message touched Jesse's heart so deeply that he went into the bathroom because he did not want his wife to see him cry. He prayed, "God, whatever Billy said." Immediately the Holy Spirit came into him, and he began to change.

One of the first things he did was give away all his money. He thought that was what you were supposed to do, and he was willing. He left his music career. He walked away from everything he thought he wanted in this world to follow Jesus. He was called to be an evangelist and has affected lives all over the world. Since then, the Lord has returned his wealth, but he continues to follow Jesus in everything.

Notes

_____

_____

_____

_____

_____

_____

_____

_____

_____

_____

_____

_____

_____

_____

_____

_____

_____

_____

_____

_____

_____

_____

_____

_____

_____

_____

_____

_____

_____

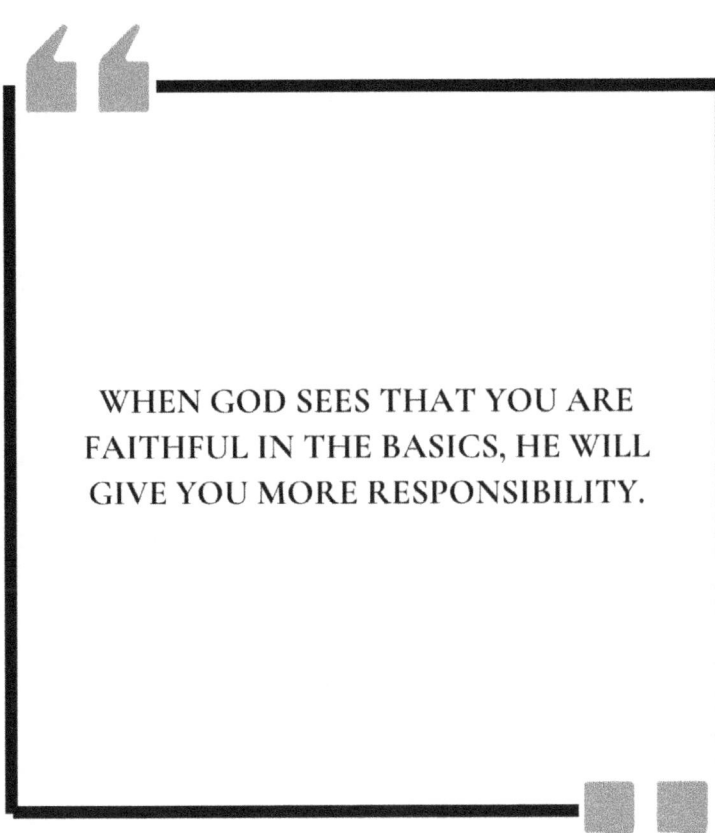

WHEN GOD SEES THAT YOU ARE
FAITHFUL IN THE BASICS, HE WILL
GIVE YOU MORE RESPONSIBILITY.

CHAPTER 6

THE WOMAN AT THE WELL

Total Acceptance

We learn how Jesus uncovers our sin and gently draws us to Himself in the face of our shame. He does not react - He reveals.

———

There are times in each of our lives when we make a big mistake; we do something we shouldn't; we miscalculate and fail. The repercussions of those actions are often rejection and shame. People make fun of you, criticize you, or avoid you. Rejection hurts. You either learn from it and try to move on, or shame takes over your life. You figure that you have already messed up, so why bother doing things right because someone will always remind you of your past? Instead of being avoided, you avoid the people who know so you don't have to keep reliving the pain.

THE FORBIDDEN ENCOUNTER

Read John 4:1-14

Why did I label this encounter as forbidden? Because the text tells us that Jews did not interact with Samaritans. In fact, many Jews would go miles out of their way to walk around Samaria so they would not have contact with the people there. The Samaritans were descendants of Jacob who had intermarried with Gentiles and chose to worship God on Mount Gerizim instead of Mount Zion in Jerusalem. It was as if they had started a cult, first by disobedience to the Law and then by worshipping at the wrong place. As if that was not enough, Jesus was speaking alone with a woman who was not accompanied by a husband or family member. This was also frowned upon.

Jesus never did anything except by instruction from His Father (see John 5:19 and John 8:28-29), therefore, we know that He was told to meet this woman at the well. He and the disciples could have gone around Samaria, but Jesus was obedient to the Father's will. The Father knew there was a soul open to His message of love in that village. Jesus was willing to go against custom and religious sentiment to reach someone whom most Jews would have thought was unworthy. He sent the disciples to buy food so He could speak with her alone at first.

John tells us that the woman came to the well in the afternoon. By this we know that she did not want to meet the other women of the village, as they would have come in the early morning to avoid the heat. She was probably looked upon with scorn and had few or no friends. Jesus startled her by asking her to give Him a drink from the well. It was an innocent question that contained a lure to get her to converse. She gave the standard reply, but the ensuing conversation drew her in. Jesus was speaking of the spiritual concept of living water. The woman was sure He was criticizing her ancestor, Jacob. However, it was to this wanton Samaritan woman that Jesus first described giving living water that flows out of Him.

Are you aware that if you belong to Christ, you have this living water, the life of God, flowing out of you? Each of us is to be obedient to the Father to share about the love of God and the gift of His only son to whomever He directs. You may think, "I'm not a pastor or evangelist. Jesus or the apostles could share but that's not my calling." Paul said that the five ministry offices were to train us so we could do the work of the ministry (see Ephesians 4:11-12). We may not want to be rejected or made fun of by people, but we forget that there could be a positive reaction. The Samaritan woman pushed back at first, but Jesus kept going. There is a saying that "You may be the only Jesus people ever see." What if having an encounter with God for a specific person means they encounter you?

STUDY QUESTIONS

Are you willing to follow the example of Jesus and witness to whomever the Father shows you? How would you handle it if that person were an outcast?

_____
_____
_____
_____
_____
_____
_____
_____
_____
_____
_____

Prepare for a future opportunity by writing what you might say to someone you know.

_____
_____
_____
_____
_____
_____
_____
_____
_____
_____
_____

WHAT IS WORSHIP?

Read John 4:15-29

I see this recounting in John like a fishing trip. In the first section, Jesus put out the bait. The thought of water so wonderful that she would never thirst again made the Samaritan woman ask for it. She took the bait, and instead of telling her how to get the water, He asked for her husband. She truthfully replied that she was not married. Then Jesus set the hook. With a word of knowledge from the Holy Spirit, He told her about her five husbands and that she was currently living with a man to whom she was not married. Can you imagine the shock and surprise on her face? I can see her immediately pulling back because her sin had been exposed. In defense, she threw out a religious argument that the Jews and Samaritans had been having for decades: "Where do you worship God?" Jesus began slowly reeling her in. He gave her one of the secrets of the Kingdom: It is not the place you worship God that matters; it is *how* you worship. God desires His children to worship Him truly from their spirits.

We still have religious disagreements over how we should worship. Older generations often think it has to be in a church with an organ, a robed choir, and a hymnal. A younger generation may roll their eyes at those old-fashioned ideas and swear that now God only likes loud worship teams with guitars, drums, screens, and jeans in a modern or outdoor setting. This is just like Jesus telling the woman that the mountain doesn't matter. When you are worshipping the Lord from your heart, it can be through a hymn or a chorus. You could hear either an organ or a guitar. It could be in a church or a stadium. There may be a choir or a praise team—or you may be by yourself. We need to stop telling each other that only certain types of music, instruments, buildings, etc., are acceptable. If you have a humble heart focused on Him, and are full of gratitude and praise, the Lord receives your worship. What accompanies it doesn't matter.

Going further, worship itself does not specifically refer to music. There may be music when you worship, but not necessarily. Several Bible translations tell us in Romans 12:1 that offering ourself as living sacrifice is worship.

It seems that the Holy Spirit drew the woman through the teaching of Jesus because she brought up the subject of the Messiah. Whatever differences there were between the Samaritans and Jews, they were both looking for the Anointed One to come. Interestingly, she said, "When he comes, he will explain everything to us," (see John 4:25 NIV). The Pharisees wanted the Messiah to come as a conqueror; she understood that He would be a teacher. Jesus put her in the fishing basket, the Kingdom, with His revelation that He is the Messiah. This is evident because she ignored the arriving disciples and ran back to the village. She overlooked the past glares, snide remarks, and avoidances, and told the whole town that she believed she had found the Messiah. If we have been Christians for a while, we must be careful not to prejudge others who have lived less than stellar lives. Just like Jesus, we must see past the sordid actions and look to the wounded heart. God loves us all and will give every opportunity for a person to turn to Him. He works in everyone who gives Him any possibility. Sometimes we must be like the disciples and stay out of the way of the working of the Holy Spirit. We don't put up obstacles; we break down barriers.

On the other side, if you identify with the Samaritan woman, with many moral or behavioral failures in your past, you can come to Jesus without fear of rejection. He sought this woman out because God loved her and wanted to offer her salvation. That is how the Lord sees each of us. He is willing to wipe out our past rebellion if we will come to Him in faith and repentance. His love drives Him to seek us out and show us unmerited mercy and grace.

STUDY QUESTIONS

Describe whether you are more like the religious Jews who avoid sinners or the Samaritan woman who realizes her need for the Savior.

_____

_____

_____

_____

_____

_____

_____

_____

_____

_____

How do you worship the Lord in spirit and in truth?

_____

_____

_____

_____

_____

_____

_____

_____

_____

_____

_____

_____

_____

KINGDOM NUTRIENTS AND A HARVEST

Read John 4:29-38

I find it interesting that none of the disciples mentioned the woman who ran away. Perhaps, knowing that people often had varying reactions to Jesus, they decided not to ask and chose to focus on the food instead. It was good that they were concerned with His wellbeing, but once again Jesus says the unexpected. "I have food to eat that you know nothing about," (see John 4:32, NIV). The Passion Translation (TPT) says, "I have eaten a meal you don't know about." In the footnotes for TPT it says, "There is a fascinating word play here in the Aramaic. The word Jesus used isn't the common word for "food," but a specific word that means "nutrients." It also has a homonym more commonly translated "kingdom." Jesus is saying that He feeds His spirit by doing the will of the Father to build the Kingdom. He is teaching the disciples that listening to the Father and obeying His directions brings spiritual health and strength. The disciples would not have suggested ministering to a town in Samaria. There were lost souls there, though, who would listen to the Gospel. Sometimes God directs us to us go beyond our comfort zone in ministry to help us grow and to reach the seemingly unreachable.

Just before this conversation, John 4:29-30 says that not only did the Samaritan woman tell everyone she saw about Jesus, but they *believed* her! What was it about her message that caused the people to drop what they were doing and go to the well to see Jesus? The obvious reason is because she claimed to have found the Messiah. But if you remember that this woman normally stayed away from people and tried to hide her shame, you realize that this behavior is totally out of character for her. Surely something amazing must have happened and the people were curious. I also believe the Holy Spirit was at work, urging them to discover the truth of the matter for themselves.

The Passion Translation begins John 4:35 with words the translators felt should be understood because of the context. *"As the crowds emerged from the village, Jesus said to his disciples..."* It helps us to understand that Jesus was referring to the Samaritans when He began to talk about the harvest. Because Jesus obeyed the Father, there was a harvest of souls that day. We need to be aware of situations in which we may be called upon to be the reapers. We may not have plowed the field or planted or watered the seeds, but God gives us the privilege of gathering the fruit of the labor of others. Likewise, sometimes we are plowing fields or planting seeds, and others will reap the harvest. We should not be discouraged when someone doesn't immediately confess Jesus as Lord. Sensitivity to the Holy Spirit is paramount in building the Kingdom of God. Here, all it took was the testimony of one woman's encounter with Jesus to shake up an entire village. Boldness came upon her, and she became the first New Testament evangelist to win a town!

STUDY QUESTIONS

What has God challenged you to do that has helped you grow?

_____

_____

_____

_____

_____

_____

_____

_____

_____

_____

_____

_____

Describe a time when you either planted a seed of the Word, or harvested a soul into the Kingdom:

_____

_____

_____

_____

_____

_____

_____

_____

_____

_____

_____

_____

ACCEPTANCE BRINGS MULTIPLICATION

Read John 4:39-42

Jesus pointed out the woman's sin, but He did not accuse her with it. Like the woman caught in adultery (see John 8:3-31), He replaced condemnation with teaching and acceptance. His love set her free and gave her the courage to share her good news with others. Many townspeople believed Jesus was the Messiah because He told the woman He knew what she had done and told her that God would still receive her worship. After teaching them for two days, many more people believed in Him. They did not just call him Messiah; they declared Him to be the Savior of the World! This was more perceptive than the Jewish religious rulers. They could not—or did not—want to see Jesus for who He truly is. It was a woman who was willing to let go of the shame of her past and boldly confess Jesus that helped to gather the harvest of many souls for the Kingdom.

MODERN EXAMPLE: JERRIANN SAVELLE

By her own admission, Jerriann messed up her life. She grew up in a family of faith, but the enemy convinced her that she wasn't worth love. After her first marriage failed, she was driven into a works-based lifestyle, showing a godly life on the outside but struggling with shame and rejection on the inside. Before she could be rejected again, she had an affair, which ended her second marriage. She felt she was the child of a famous preacher who did everything wrong. God certainly could not want her, much less use her. She stayed away from people who knew her family so she wouldn't face the stares and snide remarks, not to mention the outright accusations. Her life was going nowhere.

Through the love, acceptance, and prayers of her family, Jerriann finally had her own encounter with Jesus. She saw the lies of the enemy that had caused her to make bad choices. She saw the love of Jesus that sent Him to the cross to take the punishment for her sin so she would not have to take it. She realized that God had a plan for her life and had not given up on her. His love overcomes any obstacles.

Jerriann is now sold out to Jesus. She has a ministry and preaches wherever she can, especially to women. Her message contains the encouragement to push away shame, rejection, and fear, and stand in faith on the Word of God. The Lord has given her the courage to not let her past shape her future. Because she is willing to be used by the Lord, many people are encouraged, healed, and coming to Christ.[1]

---

1. "Happy to be Me" and "Living Unashamed" by Jerriann Savelle www.jerriann.org

Notes

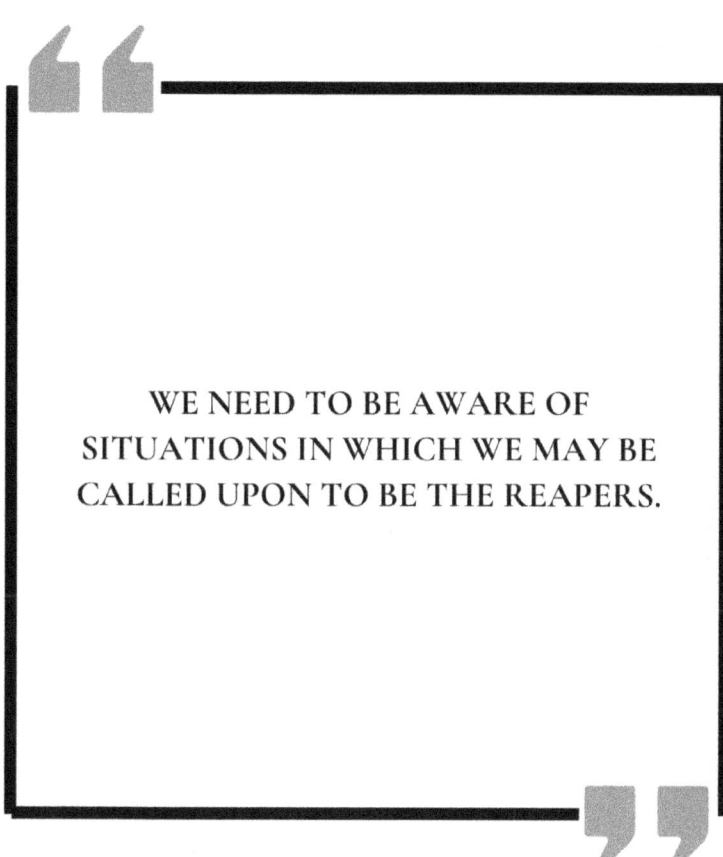

WE NEED TO BE AWARE OF
SITUATIONS IN WHICH WE MAY BE
CALLED UPON TO BE THE REAPERS.

CHAPTER 7

JAIRUS AND THE WOMAN WITH THE ISSUE OF BLOOD

Radical Faith

A side-by-side comparison of two miracles that happened together.

———

I wanted to write this chapter on just the woman with the issue of blood, but as I read the entire story again, the Lord began opening my eyes to a connection between her story and that of Jairus—and the amazing differences. If someone asked you to describe radical faith, what would you say? These two people encountered Jesus on the same day by different means, with different reactions, but similar, and wonderful, results.

We will read the entire passage and then go back to zero in on the separate accounts. I hope you see things in this study that stir up your faith for your own healing encounter.

A TYPICAL DAY IN JESUS' NEIGHBORHOOD

Read Mark 5:21-43

This passage takes place immediately after Jesus and the disciples return home from a trip across the Lake of Galilee to the Gadarenes, where Jesus had driven demons from a man and sent them into a herd of pigs. It was a hard trip and Jesus did not have time to go home and get a shower or take a nap. A crowd formed as Jesus and the disciples disembarked from the boat. Jairus quickly approached them and begged Jesus to come heal his daughter. Despite being tired from His trip, Jesus went with Jairus to his home. He didn't even get to complete that miracle before He was involved in another.

We know that many of the accounts in the gospels take place at different times and aren't usually connected, but these two miracles are intricately entwined. One happened on the way to the other. Jairus approached Jesus boldly to His face and stated his case. The woman had been looking for Jesus and may not have known that He was on the way to Jairus' home. She had heard Jesus was in town, saw the crowd, and went for the stealth approach. It was an interruption of one miracle to fulfill another. I believe that not even the timing was by chance. Later I will share why. Jesus was not thrown off by either contact. He had the heart of God and was ready to do whatever was necessary to complete His Father's will.

One of the similarities between the two accounts is the number 12. The daughter of Jairus was 12 years old. The woman with the issue of blood had been ill for 12 years. What is God saying to us by the fact that both the interwoven miracles dealt with 12 years? This happens nowhere else in the gospels.

In the Bible, the number 12 refers to God's foundation of

governance. There were 12 tribes of Israel and 12 disciples of Jesus. Our lives are counted by years comprised of 12 months. There are 24 hours in a day—12 hours a.m. and 12 hours p.m. There are 60 seconds in one minute and 60 minutes in one hour—12 x 5 = 60. Three times four is 12. God shows Himself in the Trinity. The earth has four cardinal directions. There are four gospels. God created the earth and inspired the gospel writers. I see 12 inherent in those facts. The Kingdom of God is established in order. God has no random chaotic acts. The daughter of Jairus had 12 years of life and was at the point of death. The woman had 12 years of a kind of death as she, by Jewish law, was not to be around others and had been reduced to poverty. She was at the point of a new life. It's as though satan was trying to mock the heart of God to bring healing and life. The Father showed His supremacy by responding to the faith of the woman and that of Jairus, and emphasized His order for those who will believe and follow Him.

The second similarity is that, though in different ways, they were each very determined to get a miracle from the power that came from Jesus. They focused on a goal, an intended end, and did not let anyone get in the way of their receiving. One faced Jesus with faith, the other came from behind with faith. The main ingredient in any miracle is faith in the power and promise of God. Whether you come to him quietly or boldly is of no consequence. Jesus said it is God's will to heal and it is our faith that receives the healing.

STUDY QUESTIONS

Which is your favorite account of healing in the gospels and why?

_____

_____

_____

_____

_____

_____

_____

Describe a time when you were moved by compassion to help someone despite being busy or tired.

_____

_____

_____

_____

What teaching have you heard on the meaning of numbers in the Bible?

_____

_____

_____

_____

_____

_____

A FATHER'S LOVE

Read Mark 5:21-24, 35-43

We do not know what was wrong with her, but the daughter of Jairus lay at the point of death. The minute Jairus heard people talking in the street that Jesus was back, he rushed out of his house. We know this father was desperate because he pushed his way through the crowd until he was in front of Jesus. Jairus was a synagogue leader, yet he humbled himself at the feet of Jesus. He made a request that was a plea but not a question. It was a statement of faith. *"Come and lay your hands on her and heal her and she will live!"* (see Mark 5:23 TPT).

Many times Jesus would ask petitioners, "What would you have me do for you?" He wanted them to know that they would receive according to their faith. Jairus was in a hurry, so he made his statement right up front with faith-filled words. It reminds me of Hebrews 4:16 (NKJV), "Let us therefore come boldly to the throne of grace, that we may obtain mercy and find grace to help in time of need." Jesus responded to that faith and immediately went with him.

Now we come to the sticky-wicket in the situation. Time was of the essence, but Jesus stopped because he felt power go out of Him for another healing. These were tense moments as Jesus stood looking for the person who was able to use faith alone, without His words or action. Jairus probably walked a few feet before realizing the crowd had stopped and Jesus was no longer next to him. I can imagine him frantically looking backwards and thinking, "No! What is going on? We must hurry!" Being a parent, I know it would be difficult to wait for the interruption to be handled. However, we are never given another word out of Jairus' mouth. Whatever he felt inside, he said nothing.

Precious moments were spent, and time ran out. The last words of Jesus to the woman coincided with people coming from Jairus' house to tell him his daughter had died. Before Jairus could wail and mourn and speak something counter to his faith, Jesus told him not to fear and continue in faith. Jairus was obedient. Jesus kicked all the mourners out of the house to stop the death talk. He only took three disciples and the parents into the girl's room, and He fulfilled the faith request of her father.

What a picture to us about how important our words are to our prayers being answered! You may start out in faith, but when there is a delay, do you continue to speak words of faith? Do you change your words to reflect what is happening in the physical world, or do you choose to agree with the Word of God? Do you get jealous when someone else's prayer is answered and you are still waiting? This account is one to encourage us when we see a delay in our prayers. Even when it seems time is running out, we can continue in faith because we know God is outside of time and can work despite its constraints in our natural world.

STUDY QUESTIONS

Describe your reaction to a delay in answered prayer.

_____
_____
_____
_____
_____
_____
_____
_____
_____
_____
_____

What would you say as you come boldly before God for a request?

_____
_____
_____
_____
_____
_____
_____
_____
_____
_____
_____

THE RESULTS OF NEW TESTAMENT SELF-TALK

Read Mark 5:25-34

The Bible doesn't say whether this woman lived in Capernaum or had traveled there. It says she was in the crowd that pressed around Jesus. By Jewish law, if you had an issue of blood or if you touched someone with an issue of blood, you were unclean (see Exodus 15:25-27). She knew that by going out into that crowd, she would be making anyone who touched her unclean. She must have been incredibly desperate to do such a thing. Wouldn't you be desperate if you had spent every penny you had on doctors and, after 12 years, nothing had changed? What was it that drove her desperation to action?

Mark 5:27-28 (AMPC) says, "She heard the reports concerning Jesus, and she came up behind Him in the throng and touched His garment, for she kept saying, 'If I only touch His garments, I shall be restored to health.'" Is it possible that she did not want to make Jesus unclean, so she chose to only touch His prayer shawl (tallit)? This shawl had fringe on the short ends, with a long fringe at each corner that had a knot in it. She had heard of His healing power and thought that if she could even touch just one long fringe, there would be enough power to heal her. She would not have to face Him with her shame, and no one would know.

I also put these verses here in the Amplified Classic version because it translates a Greek word to its correct tense. "She *kept saying*." The Passion Translation says, "She kept saying to herself...." Over and over, the woman said in her thoughts, and probably sometimes out loud, "If I only touch his garment, I will be healed." Between what she heard others say about Jesus and what she told herself about Him, faith came. This is a great example of the principle Paul wrote about in Romans 10:17: "Faith comes by hearing." Her faith that she would be healed became so strong that she did not worry about what others would think if she were caught; the results were worth the action.

Isn't it amazing that many people were touching Jesus that day, but only the woman was healed? Surely there were others around Him who needed miracles. The fact that someone pulled power out of Him without first asking was so astonishing to Jesus that He stopped following Jairus to speak with that person. He did not want to scold but encourage. When He asked who touched Him, any number of people nearby could have answered "I did." The question confused everyone except the woman who came before Him, fell at His feet, and confessed. I believe that Jesus gently but soundly confirmed to her, and everyone who had ears to hear, that it was her faith in the power of God coming through Him that healed her. He told her to go in peace and spoke wholeness to her entire being. Since "peace" can also mean "prosperity," it is possible that God made a way for her money to be restored. He said that she should be free from suffering. She was not only suffering physically, but she also suffered financially. God wants us whole in every area of life.

This nameless woman has been remembered in the gospels and preached about all over the world because she chose to act in faith. We should do the same.

STUDY QUESTIONS

What issue in your life would drive you to be aggressive in faith, even at the risk of embarrassment?

_____

_____

_____

_____

_____

_____

_____

_____

_____

_____

Describe whether you are more like the woman, who was ready to receive, or the crowd, who just wanted to be close to the action.

_____

_____

_____

_____

_____

_____

_____

_____

_____

_____

_____

FAITH AND ACTION

Read Hebrews 11:1 and James 2:14-26

All the people we have studied have had faith. We see it repeatedly in stories about biblical characters. Does it work in our own lives? If not, we need to understand why. Hebrews 11:1 defines faith. Depending on the Bible translation, faith is described as the substance, confidence, assurance, or even the title deed of what we hope for—which is evidence of things that cannot be seen. This makes the word *faith* an abstract noun. It is a concept, not something concrete that you can see. However, according to James 2:14-26, you can see the results of it.

When Jesus talked to Nicodemus in John 3:8, He spoke of the wind. You can't see the wind; you can only hear it or see the action it takes, like leaves moving in trees. Likewise, you can't see faith. James tells us we know where faith is by the actions it engenders. Jairus and the woman put action to their faith. They both came to Jesus and they both spoke words of faith, not words of confusion or doubt. James wrote about Abraham, who put action to his faith in the promises of God by obeying instructions. We show our faith by our words and deeds. Does your faith seem to not be working? Check what you are doing or saying on a regular basis. Do you continue with your "faith talk" even when the answer takes longer than you expect? We should walk by faith in the unseen assurance of God, not by sight, what we see physically around us. Repeat God's promises from the Bible because "faith comes by hearing," and you believe what *you* say the most.

STUDY QUESTIONS

Describe a time when you put action to your faith.

_____
_____
_____
_____
_____
_____
_____
_____

When have you noticed yourself or someone else make a faith statement, but act or speak contrary to it afterwards?

_____
_____
_____
_____
_____
_____
_____
_____

Which of the two accounts we discussed speaks to you more and why?

_____
_____
_____
_____
_____
_____
_____
_____

MODERN EXAMPLES: DODIE OSTEEN AND ANDREW WOMMACK

Dodie Osteen:

At the age of 48, after 20 days of being in the hospital for multiple tests, Dodie was diagnosed with metastatic cancer of the liver. The doctor told her husband John that she had only weeks to live. He wanted to start chemotherapy right away, but John told the doctor they believed in miracles. He would take Dodie home to pray. That was December 10th. On December 11th, they got on their faces before God. They quoted the promises of God concerning healing and Dodie declared that she received complete healing of liver cancer on that day.

Nothing visible changed for quite a while. She was tired and sick, and at times had abnormal bleeding. However, she did as much work as she could, including ministering to other people. Even though she was in great pain, when someone asked her how she was doing, she would reply that she was blessed, and that she had received her healing on December 11th. It took months before she began to feel well.

Like the woman with the issue of blood who kept saying to herself, "If I just touch the hem of his garment, I will be healed," Dodie spoke the Word for healing. Every day she quoted 40 healing scriptures. No matter how she felt, she declared those scriptures and the date she received her healing.[1] She continues to read those scriptures every day of her life. In October of 2023 she will be 90 years old.

———

Andrew Wommack:

After an international ministry trip, Andrew and his wife

Jamie arrived home late at night. A few hours later their oldest son called to tell them their youngest son, Peter, had died. Andrew boldly declared, "The first report is not the last report!" He and Jamie took authority and commanded life back into Peter. During the hour-long trip to the hospital, they worshipped and praised God. They did not speak words of worry, doubt, fear, or grief.

At the hospital, their oldest son told them that 5 to 10 minutes after they spoke, Peter sat up! He had been taken to the hospital morgue and put in a cooler with a toe tag. His body was discolored because it had been between four and five hours since he was declared dead. Andrew and Jamie prayed over him, and God raised him from the dead![2] Because of their faith, bold declarations, and refusing to accept what they were told, their son is alive today.

---

1. https://www.youtube.com/watch?v=52IaLDgiz0I
2. https://www.youtube.com/watch?v=8UIx5uVzVfI&t=250s

Notes

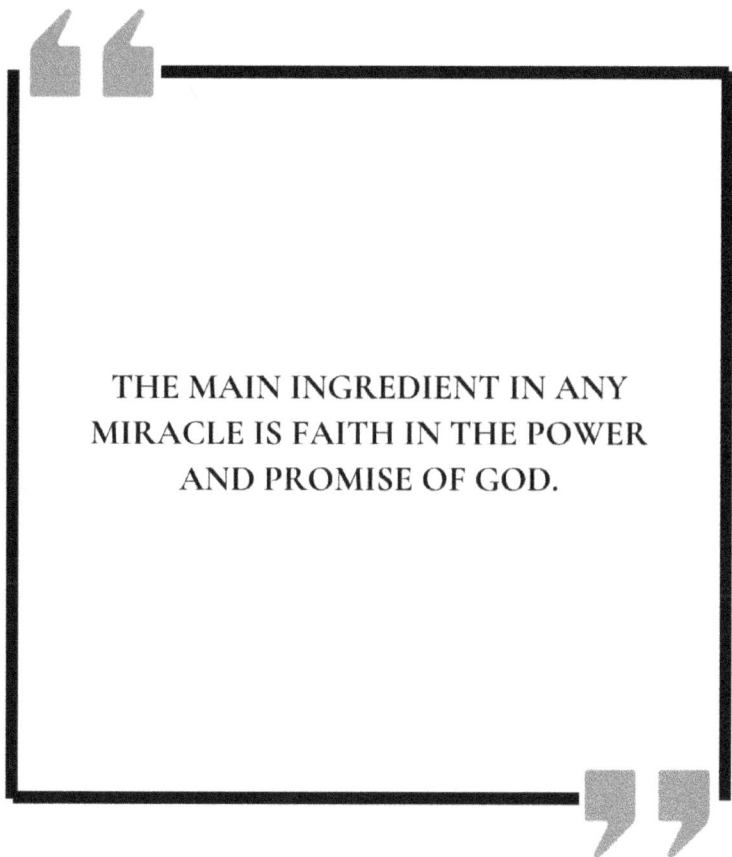

THE MAIN INGREDIENT IN ANY
MIRACLE IS FAITH IN THE POWER
AND PROMISE OF GOD.

CHAPTER 8

PAUL

True Repentance

Within moments of being struck down, a zealot for the Law of Moses became a zealot for the Love of God.

Studying the entire life of Paul would take some time. Although he was not one of the original 12 disciples, he was the most prolific. We base a great deal of our faith doctrines on his revelations from Jesus. Those would be interesting to discuss here, but they are not the focus for this chapter.

Paul had many encounters with Jesus. We will study two at the beginning of his ministry. Most of us have heard accounts of sinners who met Jesus and turned their lives around. We easily understand that when an evil person repents, they go from being in the kingdom of darkness to being in the kingdom of light. Paul, though, was a fierce protector of the laws of God. We will dig into why his change after his encounters with Jesus was also a display of repentance.

WHO WAS PAUL?

Read Philippians 3:4-6, Galatians 1:13-14, and Acts 8:1-3

Paul's birth name was Saul, and he came from the city of Tarsus. His father's family was from the tribe of Benjamin, and he was raised as a Pharisee. The Pharisees were a part of a council of men from all walks of life. They believed that the oral laws which were passed down through generations were just as important as the written Law of Moses. For them, the oral traditions helped interpret the books of Moses and gave instructions for daily living. They also believed in the resurrection of the dead.

In the above verses, we hear from Paul himself how strictly he kept the Law. His zeal for the Word of God and adherence to the standards of living were higher than those of other Jews. He was a defender of the faith in his own thinking. According to Jewish tradition, he likely had most of the first five books of the Old Testament memorized. It was very important to him that Jews kept the tenets of their beliefs to separate them from the pagan cultures around them. Today we might describe him as someone who keeps the letter of the law but not the spirit of it.

Saul had a fervor to satisfy rules and regulations. Nowhere did he say that he knew the heart or love of God. There are many "Sauls" in the body of Christ today who prefer to zero in on the faults of others, as though those faults would cause someone to be rejected by God. In contrast, these same "Sauls" believe their adherence to the Law—what they do and don't do—makes them closer to God. I'm not saying we should tolerate sin. However, we should remain humble and not put others down to make ourselves look better. According to Romans 3:23 NIV, "All have sinned and fall short of the glory of God." Yes, God has rules, but He would rather you follow them out of love for Him, than out of fear of punishment, or to be better than anyone else.

The fervor of Saul for Jewish rules and traditions drove him to seek to destroy the new sect of Judaism called "The Way." People of this sect broke traditions and worshiped their leader, who claimed to be the Messiah—*blasphemy*! Saul approved of the murder of Stephen and then began a relentless persecution of the church. He led a group that dragged men and women out of their houses to be put in prison. It is believed that a number of these people were executed. Saul was so blinded by his passion for man-made rules that He missed how Jesus fulfilled the promises and prophecies of the Old Testament. He could not see the love of God being demonstrated in the healings and miracles. Saul's heart was cold to the message Stephen preached before he was martyred.

Have you ever been so used to man-made rules that you took it as a personal affront when someone came to your church and broke them without realizing it? *Did that person just sit in Mrs. Smith's pew? They were singing too loudly and raising their hands! Why would they wear something like that to church*! Once while I was preaching in a small country church, I started to get irritated by a visitor who wouldn't get off his cell phone (most of my congregation was older and did not bring cell phones to church). While I continued speaking, I thought, "Can't he wait until after the service to text his friends?" Yes, I was on my religious high horse. I later found out he was so impressed by my sermon that he was taking notes! I was glad I had not complained to anyone so I could eat my humble pie quietly.

Saul outwardly appeared to be a very righteous Jew, but in his heart, he was as far from God as most sinners. "People look at the outward appearance, but the Lord looks at the heart."

(see 1 Samuel 16:7 NIV) As we go through our day, we want to give our best to God. The only motive for our actions should be to please God, not others or ourselves.

STUDY QUESTIONS

Do you see yourself as a Saul? Can you identify with his zeal for perfection? Describe why or why not.

_____
_____
_____
_____
_____
_____
_____
_____
_____
_____
_____
_____

Have you ever been persecuted for the way you worship God?

_____
_____
_____
_____
_____
_____
_____
_____

SAUL'S "TAKEDOWN"

Read Acts 9:1-9

Not content to terrorize the church only in Jerusalem, Saul decided to go after the believers who lived in Damascus. Acts 9:1 in The Passion Translation says, "During those days, Saul, full of angry threats and rage, wanted to murder the disciples of the Lord Jesus." This compulsion was driven by satan, who wanted to eradicate the followers of Jesus. With the power of the Holy Spirit, news of the Messiah and new converts to Him quickly spread to countries beyond Israel. Saul obtained the proper permission and eagerly led his own followers to their prey in Damascus.

Here we see the epitome of the spirit of religion persecuting those who are led by the Holy Spirit. When I speak of "religion", I mean man-made rules to work our way to God. "Religious" people often use their good works to advance in status, or to obtain God's acceptance or love. Some use works (or deeds) to show they are more holy and righteous than others. Ephesians 2:10 does tell us that we were created to do good works, but Ephesians 4:12 (NIV) explains why: "...to equip his people for works of service, so that the body of Christ may be built up...." Our good works (or deeds, as Paul frequently wrote in the Epistles) should be done out of a heart of love for God and His people. They should be done to serve others, not our own agenda.

God wanted to take Saul's zeal and focus it in the right direction. Since he wasn't moved by listening to Stephen, it was obvious that subtle hints weren't going to get his attention. Jesus appeared to Saul in a brilliant light and spoke in an audible voice. The men with him heard the voice but saw nothing. The power of the Holy Spirit knocked Saul to the ground. How do you imagine he felt when the voice said, "I am Jesus, whom you are persecuting"? I can imagine a number of thoughts that may have bombarded Saul's mind. *Wait, Jesus? I thought He was killed. Did God really raise Him from the dead? I'm not persecuting Him. Is He talking about His followers? Who will tell me what to do?* When Saul stood and tried to look around, the blindness in his heart manifested in his eyes. His spiritual condition was being shown to him. He suffered for three days before relief came, but I am sure the Holy Spirit was speaking to him. Since he was unable to carry out his own religious purpose, Jesus was able to instruct him in the true ways of the Father.

There may be times when you think God is punishing you. Perhaps it is a season where God wants you to stop pursuing your plans and listen for His. This is different than an attack from the enemy. God does not want to harm you, but He may frustrate your plans because they are leading you in a wrong direction. Even good plans are not right if they are not God's will for you. Rather than receiving a drastic measure from the Lord, take time to pray and fellowship with Him. Ask Him what His plans are for your future. Be willing to accept a change, even if it means you must give up something you care about. Obedience is always better than sacrifice, and it puts you in the place to receive blessing and increase from the Lord.

STUDY QUESTIONS

Describe a time when you were going the wrong direction and God had to turn you around.

_____

_____

_____

_____

_____

_____

_____

_____

_____

_____

_____

_____

_____

What have you given up so that you could obey an instruction from the Lord?

_____

_____

_____

_____

_____

_____

_____

_____

JUST AN ORDINARY MAN

Read Acts 9:10-19

When you read verse 10, did you notice that Ananias was described simply as a disciple (or believer, follower—depending on the Bible version)? He was not labeled "apostle," "prophet," or "teacher." That means he was not a leader in the church; he was a member of the congregation. It was to him that the Lord appeared in a vision. He received the instruction to find and pray for Saul, who was to become one of the most well-known men of the Bible. The Lord did not choose an apostle or a prophet for this task. He chose a person who would listen and obey. Although Ananias pushed back a little because he had heard of Saul and knew why he was in Damascus, when the Lord explained, he went. He left fear behind and stepped out in faith.

It cannot be stressed enough that God needs *every* believer in the body of Christ to be listening and obedient to Him. We *all* have His power and authority to do good works, not just the "big guys." In fact, many in the Church have shirked the collective responsibility to be salt and light in the earth by leaving most of the spreading of the Gospel to the five ministry offices. Ephesians 4:12 in The Passion Translation says, "And their calling is to nurture and prepare all the holy believers to do their own works of ministry, and as they do this they will enlarge and build up the body of Christ." Today, the apostle, prophet, evangelist, pastor, and teacher are the professors in the college of Jesus. Yes, they go around and do some works, but their main function is to teach the Body of Christ to minister! This includes *you*! Ananias' encounter should serve as an example to you. You can have visions; you can hear the voice of God! Helping with your church's food pantry or donating to a mission project is good, but what about the lady in the grocery store who is limping? What about your next-door neighbor whose child is on drugs? What about the unbelieving family member who is in the hospital? These are the times and places that you are to minister the Good News of Jesus. God may even show you a vision of someone who needs help. The Holy Spirit desires to work *with* you to reach your world and He has many ways to do it—if you will make yourself available!

Saul's second encounter happened during those three days that he was blind and fasting. Although we are only told of the vision in which he saw Ananias coming to pray for him, I believe the Holy Spirit spoke to Saul more than once. It is possible that Saul was going over the scriptures about the Messiah in his mind and the Holy Spirit explained to him how Jesus fulfilled all of them. He previously had great zeal to keep the rules and regulations of Judaism but had no words from the Lord. After Saul's spiritual sight was opened through visions and instruction, Ananias prayed for him, and his natural sight was also restored.

Several times in my life, I have heard some version of the question, "Who taught Billy Graham the way to salvation? Did that person know what an impact their obedience would have on the world?" There are probably only a few people today who have the answer to that question, but for most of us it is unknown. Even so, that person had a part in spreading the gospel to millions of people through simple obedience to a call to minister. Saul was to become Paul, the great evangelist, apostle, prophet, and teacher. He was helped by a regular church member—a believer who was willing to answer and obey when God spoke. I wonder if Ananias understood what impact his actions would have on the world.

STUDY QUESTIONS

Do you believe it is only the pastor's job to bring people into the church? Why or why not?

_____

_____

_____

_____

_____

_____

_____

_____

_____

_____

Write about a time you obeyed the Lord to minister to someone.

_____

_____

_____

_____

_____

_____

_____

_____

_____

_____

FROM DARKNESS TO LIGHT

Read Acts 9:20-30

Wow! Saul went to Damascus to imprison and possibly kill Christians, and within a few days he was preaching *with* them! The footnotes of The Passion Translation point us to the Aramaic version of the New Testament, which says this occurred within an hour after regaining his sight and breaking his fast. With his newfound understanding of Jesus, Saul wasted no time in putting his zeal to God's purpose. Think of it as if a lawyer suddenly went from being the prosecutor to being an attorney for the defense—in the middle of the trial. Wouldn't that cause an uproar in the courtroom?

I mentioned before that Saul went from spiritual and physical darkness to light. He later wrote to the church at Colosse that God "…rescued us from the kingdom of darkness and transferred us into the Kingdom of His dear Son," (see Colossians 1:13 NLT). The reason I believe that the Holy Spirit was teaching Saul during those 3 days is because we see his immediate ability to preach that Jesus is the Messiah. Saul was shown the light of the Truth and he was able to "connect the dots," so to speak. When he was living in spiritual darkness, he could not see the Truth. The bright light from heaven that knocked him to the ground turned his world on its head. He went from the darkness of deception to the light of The Word. He was powerful before with the backing of the high priest. Afterward, he baffled the Jews because he grew more powerful. The Holy Spirit gave him the words to prove Jesus is the Messiah.

I want to explain why I titled this chapter "True Repentance." To repent does not mean to feel sorry for what you did. That is regret. When you repent you make a 180 degree turn in the way you live; you go the opposite direction, you choose a new path. If you are not following the path of God, the path of life, you need to repent. You are following a path of death. We recognize when some people are on that path if they are doing things like lying, cheating, stealing, having any kind of sexual relation that is not within the covenant of marriage, or overtly following the enemy. What we may not easily recognize is when we are living religiously with our own agenda, not walking in love, not being humble, or rewriting scripture to fit our theology. Jesus told the religious leaders that they were like white-washed tombs. They outwardly followed some of God's rules, but their hearts did not belong to God, and they made up their own regulations. Saul was one of those. We must examine our hearts to see whether we truly love God and follow Him, or whether we are just playing a part. If you do not obey His instructions and commands, you do not love Jesus. Repent; turn around. The Holy Spirit will immediately connect your spirit with the life of God. You will worship in spirit and in truth.

STUDY QUESTIONS

**Is there any part of Saul's life that you identify with?
Why or why not?**

_____

_____

_____

_____

_____

_____

_____

_____

**Have you truly repented of your sin to follow Jesus?
How did your life turn around?**

_____

_____

_____

_____

_____

_____

_____

_____

MODERN EXAMPLE: MARIA WOODWORTH-ETTER

Maria was born on July 22, 1844, the 4th daughter of eight children. She was born again when she was 13 years old and felt God had called her to be an evangelist. Maria did not persecute believers, but she did resist the call of God. She said that she wanted to go but many things held her back. Her father had died two years earlier, and she and her older sisters had to work to help support the family. She felt uneducated, even though she tried to study on her own. Most churches would not allow women preachers at that time, so she thought she should marry a Christian man and go on the mission field. A few years later she married P. H. Woodworth.

Even though she'd had visions of the Lord and of Heaven, Maria was fearful and timid to speak out about those things. And as it turns out, her husband did not want to be a missionary after all. Her health was bad, and five of her six children died. She finally told the Lord, "If you heal me, I will go." She recovered immediately but again struggled with fear. The Lord would show her visions of hell and the people going there who needed her to share the Gospel, but she still resisted.

She asked God to anoint her with the power of the Holy Spirit, like he had done with the apostles. Describing this, she wrote, "The power of the Holy Spirit came down as a cloud. It was brighter than the sun. I was covered and wrapped up in it. My body was light as the air. It seemed that heaven came down. I was baptized with the Holy Spirit and fire and power which has never left me."

Like Saul, this experience turned her around. She told the Lord she wanted time to study the Bible because she needed better understanding. The Lord responded by giving her a vision of a large Bible with verses in raised letters. When she looked at it, she could understand it all.

That began one of the greatest ministries of the late 19th and early 20th centuries. When she preached with power, many souls were converted. The first few years she held revivals, and when enough people were saved, she would plant a church. Then signs began to happen; people would fall under the power of the Holy Spirit, have visions, and be "frozen" where they were. In February of 1885, the Lord told her to preach divine healing, and that He had given her the gift of healing. When the healings began, her ministry exploded. She preached all over the country for more than 40 years. Her repentance led to the salvation and deliverance of many.[1]

---

1. "Signs and Wonders" by Maria Woodworth-Etter, published 1997 by Whitaker House

Notes

EVEN GOOD PLANS ARE NOT RIGHT IF
THEY ARE NOT GOD'S WILL FOR YOU.

CONCLUSION

It is my prayer, now that you have completed this study, that you understand how deeply the Creator of the Universe wants to meet with you. As we have seen, there are many ways to encounter the Lord. You don't have to be perfect. You don't have to be a professional in ministry. You simply need a heart to love and worship the Father.

I have had a number of encounters with the Lord. They have come as visions, dreams, hearing the "still small voice" within me, and, on two occasions, talking with angels. I have no special gift other than the Holy Spirit, who lives within me. He leads me in my study of scriptures and guides me during my daily life. There have been many times when I didn't listen or chose to do things my way. When I repented and confessed my sin I was always forgiven.

If you have been in church but have never fully given your life to the Lordship of Jesus Christ, I ask you to say this prayer:

> *Father God, I realize that by not giving you total control of my life, I have sinned. I have fallen short of your glorious inheritance. Today, I surrender my life to Jesus. I believe He came to the earth as a perfect man, gave His life on the cross for my healing, and went to hell for my punishment. I believe that on the third day you raised Him from the dead and gave Him the name that is above all other names. Today I declare that Jesus Christ is my Savior and Lord. Amen.*

Please let me know that you have done this by emailing info@kmjministries.com. As soon as you have the opportunity, get baptized in water. It is an outward sign of your death to self and resurrection to Life in God. I praise God for you and all the good works He has in store for you!

If you have had an encounter that you would like to share, please email the above address.
God bless you.

Kathleen Jimenez